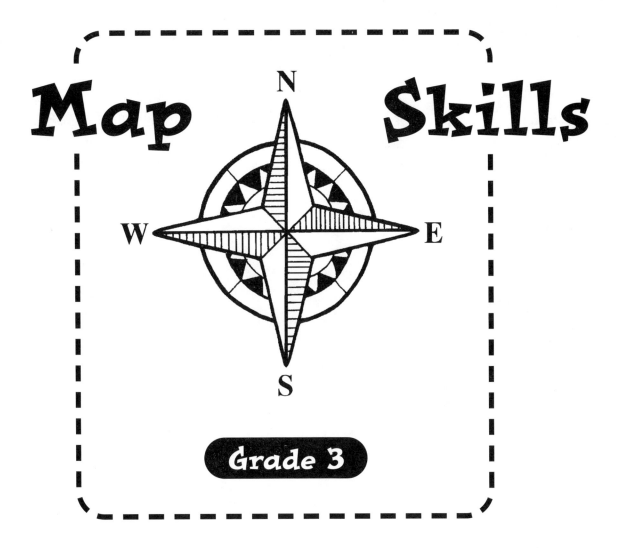

Map Skills

Grade 3

by Sharon Thompson

Carson-Dellosa Publishing Company, Inc.
Greensboro, North Carolina

Credits

Project Director
Tara Poitras

Editors
Whitney Brooks
Erin Proctor

Inside Illustrators
Milton Hall
Mike Duggins
Erik Huffine

Cover Design
Matthew Van Zomeren

Cover Photos
Mountain High Maps®
Copyright © 1993 Digital Wisdom, Inc.
Photo www.comstock.com

Special thanks to the teachers of Hamilton Elementary–Carol McMillen, Carol Griffiths, Marlys Heisler, and Lisa Gray–for their assistance with this project.

© 2003, Carson-Dellosa Publishing Company, Inc., Greensboro, North Carolina 27425. All rights reserved. The purchase of this material entitles the buyer to reproduce worksheets and activities for home or classroom use only—not for commercial resale. Reproduction of these materials for an entire school or district is prohibited. No part of this book may be reproduced (except as noted above), stored in a retrieval system, or transmitted in any form or by any means (mechanically, electronically, recording, etc.) without the prior written consent of Carson-Dellosa Publishing Co., Inc.

Printed in the USA • All rights reserved.

ISBN 0-88724-961-2

Table of Contents

Introduction 4
Jacob's Neighborhood *(compass rose)* 5
Following Directions *(compass rose)* 6
The Old West *(map key/direction)* 7
Craft Fair *(map key/floor plan)* 8
Lacey's Laundry *(floor plan)* 9
My Map *(making a map)* 10
Stargazer *(grid and coordinates)* 11
Wonder Cave *(grid and coordinates)* 12
African Safari *(map scale)* 13
How Far? *(map scale)* 14
Places Laura Lived *(reading a map)* 15
What's Your Area Code? *(reading a map/area code)* 16
Know Your State *(US state abbreviations)* 17
State Abbreviations 1 *(US state abbreviations)* 18
State Abbreviations 2 *(US state abbreviations)* 19
Zeke's Letters *(US state abbreviations)* 20
Regions of the US *(US regions)* 21
Boundaries within the US *(US boundaries)* 22
Matching Cities and States *(US cities and states)* 23
Cross-Country Cycling *(tracing a route)* 24
In Terms of Geography *(geography terms)* 25
Land Features *(geography terms)* 26
Mapping Physical Features *(physical map)* 27
Barge and Ship Traffic *(physical map)* 28
Precious Products *(product map)* 29
How's the Weather Up There? *(weather map)* 30
Zany Zones *(US time zones)* 31
Getting to Know a Globe *(globe)* 32
East and West *(hemispheres)* 33
Round and Round *(introducing latitude)* 34
Up and Down *(introducing longitude)* 35
Hailey's Report *(latitude/longitude)* 36
Jeffrey's Stamp Collection *(locating countries)* 37
Mixed-Up Continents *(continents)* 38
Cities, Countries, Continents *(cities/countries/continents)* 39
Cities and Countries *(political map)* 40
Earth's Oceans *(oceans)* 41
Matching Maps *(review)* 42
Map Skills Review *(review)* 43
Word Search *(review)* 44
Map of the United States 45
Answer Key 46

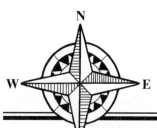

Introduction

Students may not realize it, but they use map skills every day. Walking to a friend's house and shopping at the mall both require map-skill knowledge. The activities in this book will teach students how to read maps and how to apply this knowledge to their everyday lives. Students will be introduced to a variety of map types. They will learn how to use a compass rose and map key, how to trace a route, how to measure distance on a map, and how to make maps of their own. A full-page US map with the states and capitals labeled is included in the back of the book to help with some of the activities.

Additionally, this book covers different parts of the world, as well as interesting geographical facts about the world. Students will learn just how important map skills are to them as they learn more about the world around them. The activities require thinking, drawing, and writing (and in some cases, an atlas and ruler). The activities in this book will help students develop

Make Map-Skill Lessons Come Alive!

Below is a list of activities and suggestions that can be used in addition to those included in this book. These ideas can be used as written or can be tailored to fit your classroom's needs.

1. Create hands-on maps
Be creative! Items in the classroom, kitchen, and probably the trunk of your car can make mapmaking and map-skill learning more fun and meaningful! For example, make an edible physical map from packaged sugar dough, with chocolate drop candies for mountains, blue frosting for bodies of water, etc.

2. Get students moving
Use students as "human maps" or globes. To demonstrate a map scale, have two students act as locations—such as two states— by standing at opposite ends of the classroom. Provide students with a scale so the class can determine the real distance between the two locations. Or, take students to the mall, a local park, or the playground to practice directions, map coordinates, and mapmaking.

3. Design a geo-center
Create a designated classroom center with students' projects and geography manipulatives, such as an inflatable globe, flash cards, maps, and an atlas.

4. Provide a laminated map for each student
Whether using a commercially made or a copied/laminated map, invest in maps that students can hold, write on, and refer to throughout lessons.

5. Keep a binder or pizza-box portfolio for each student
Clean pizza boxes are a great way to house map projects, reports, notes, and worksheets. Place them in the geo-center for safekeeping and convenient reference.

Name_____

compass rose

Jacob's Neighborhood

Look at the map of Jacob's neighborhood. Use the directions on the **compass rose** to fill in the blanks. North, south, east, and west are **cardinal directions**. Northeast, northwest, southeast, and southwest are **intermediate directions**.

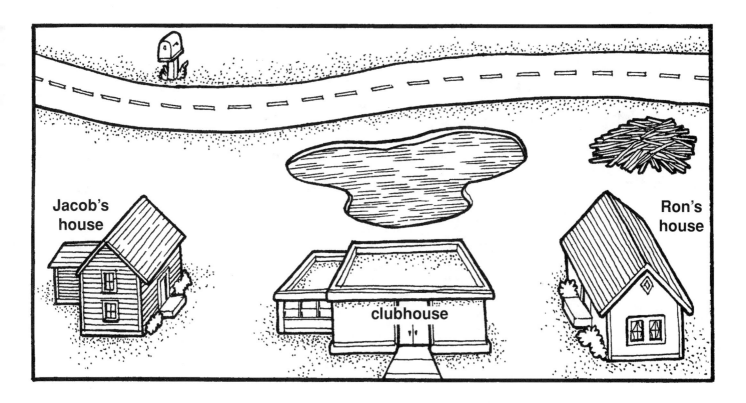

1. The pond is _____ of the clubhouse.
2. Jacob's house is _____ of the clubhouse.
3. Ron's house is _____ of the clubhouse.
4. The brush pile is _____ of the clubhouse.
5. The mailbox is _____ of the clubhouse.

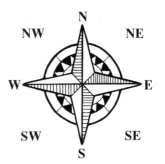

Name_____

compass rose

Following Directions

Start at the ● on the map below and follow the directions to trace a path through town. Place an X at the finishing point. The first one has been done for you.

1. Go east 2 blocks.
2. Go south 1 block.
3. Go east 2 blocks.
4. Go south 1 block.
5. Go west 1 block.
6. Go south 2 blocks.
7. Go east 1 block.
8. Go north 1 block.
9. Go east 3 blocks.
10. Go south 1 block.

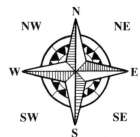

Start

Name_____

map key/direction

The Old West

Sheriff Dylan lives in the western town of Dodge. He has drawn a map and **map key** to help visitors find their way around. A map key tells what the symbols on a map represent. Use the map and map key to answer the questions below.

1. What is the symbol for the bank? _____
2. The jail is east of the _____.
3. The restaurant is north of the _____.
4. Visitors can shop at the general store, which is west of the _____.
5. Horses can sleep in the _____ _____, which are southeast of the jail.

© Carson-Dellosa CD-4702   Map Skills—Grade 3

Name_____

map key/floor plan

Craft Fair

A **floor plan** shows the layout of a house or building. The floor plan below shows the building where a craft club is having its annual fair. Use the map key and the clues below to find the rooms where projects will be judged.

Co #1	AC #1	AC #2
Co #2		
Ba #1		
Ba #2	Se #1	Se #2

Map Key
Co = cooking room
Se = sewing room
Ba = baking room
AC = arts and crafts room

1. Jami's cake will be judged in Baking Room #2.
   Mark this room with a red circle.

2. Alison has a meal to be judged in Cooking Room #1.
   Draw an orange triangle on this room.

3. David's painting is on display in Arts and Crafts Room #2.
   Mark this room with a yellow rectangle.

4. Christie has sewn a shirt. It will be judged in Sewing Room #1.
   Color this room purple.

Name_____

floor plan

Lacey's Laundry

Lacey wants to help people do their laundry. To make sure she does not mix up the laundry, Lacey created a floor plan of the laundromat. Help Lacey by filling out the floor plan. Follow the directions below.

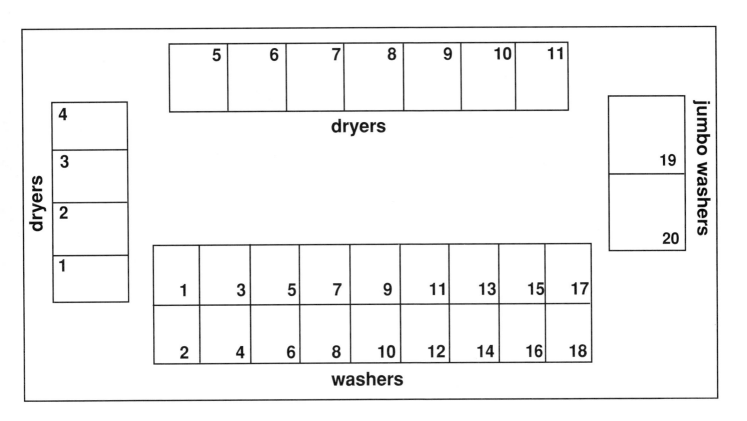

1. Mrs. Wyatt's clothes are in washer 18. Mark it with a W.
2. Mrs. Gray's blankets are in jumbo washer 20. Mark it with a G.
3. Mr. Hanson's jeans are drying in dryer 9. Mark it with an H.
4. The James family has many clothes. Mark a J on washers 2–5.
5. Mr. Sherrick sent some shirts to be washed. Mark an S on washer 13.
6. Miss Templeton's dryer broke. She has sheets in dryer 6. Mark it with a T.
7. Mrs. Blake sent her pillowcases. They are in washer 17. Mark it with a B.

Name_____

making a map

My Map

You have learned about the compass rose, map symbols, and map key. Use your knowledge to create a map of your school in the space below. Label the compass rose. If you wish, add symbols to the map key.

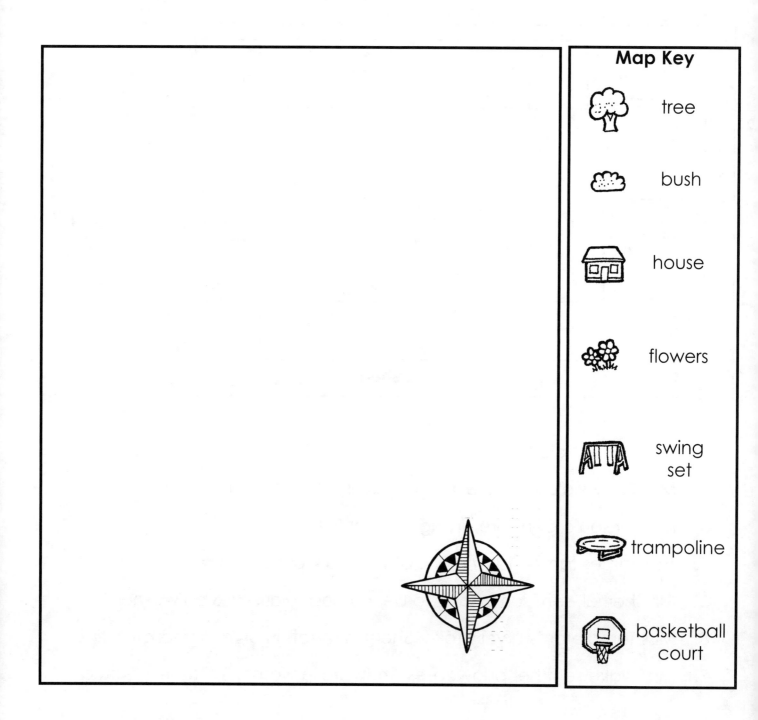

© Carson-Dellosa CD-4702
Map Skills—Grade 3

Name_____

grid and coordinates

Stargazer

A **grid** (set of lines on a map) and **coordinates** (the letters and numbers beside the grid) help locate places on a map. Cut out the **constellations** (groups of stars) and place them on the star map below. Use the coordinates given.

	1	2	3	4
E				
F				
G				

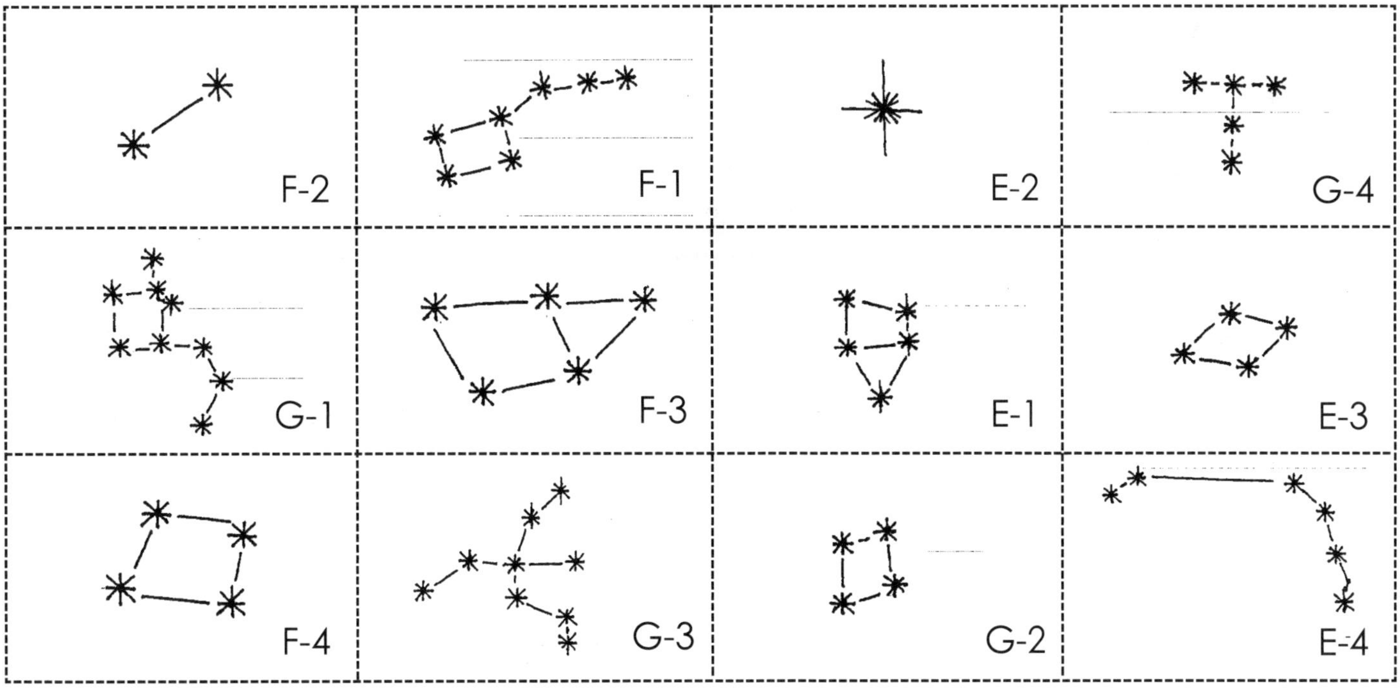

F-2	F-1	E-2	G-4
G-1	F-3	E-1	E-3
F-4	G-3	G-2	E-4

© Carson-Dellosa CD-4702

Map Skills—Grade 3

Name _____

grid and coordinates

Wonder Cave

Veronica took a trip to Wonder Cave. Use the grid and coordinates below to find out what she saw there. Write the coordinates for each item listed.

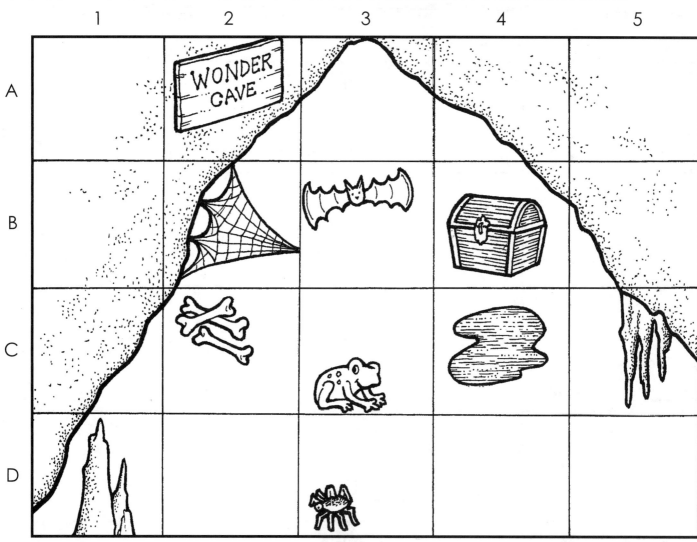

				Letter	Number
1.	The sign for Wonder Cave			____	- ____
2.	A pile of bones			____	- ____
3.	A spider near the entrance			____	- ____
4.	A toad			____	- ____
5.	The spider's web			____	- ____
6.	A flying bat			____	- ____
7.	A treasure chest			____	- ____

Name _____

map scale

African Safari

A **map scale** shows distance on a map. A map cannot be shown at actual size, so it must be made smaller to fit on paper. On the map of Africa, 1 cm = 10 kilometers. Measure the distances between the dots with a ruler. Then, change the centimeters to kilometers.

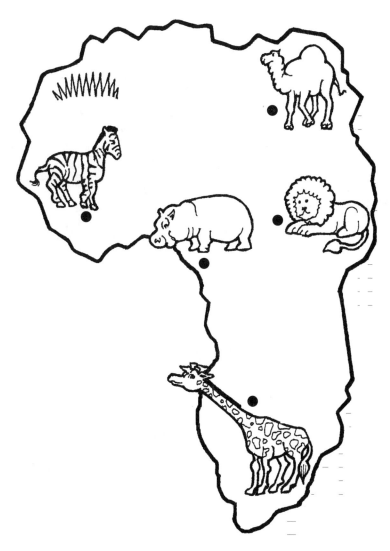

1. How far are the zebras from the lions? _____ kilometers
2. How far are the hippos from the lions? _____ kilometers
3. The camels are _____ kilometers from the giraffes.
4. The lions are _____ kilometers from the giraffes.

Name_____

map scale

How Far?

Juan's family is planning a vacation for the summer. His dad does not want to drive more than 600 miles. Using the scale and the map below, find out how far each site is from Juan's home. Answer the questions.

1 inch = 600 miles

1. Is the Grand Canyon within 600 miles of Juan's home? _____

2. Which is closer to Juan's home, the St. Louis Arch or the Baseball Hall of Fame?

   _____

3. Which is farther from Juan's home, the Space Needle or the Grand Canyon?

   _____

4. How far is Mt. Rushmore from Juan's home?

   _____

© Carson-Dellosa CD-4702

Map Skills—Grade 3

Name_____

reading a map

Places Laura Lived

Laura Ingalls Wilder wrote a famous series of books called the *Little House* books. The map below shows the places where Laura lived. Study the map and answer the questions. The numbers on the map represent the order in which Laura lived in each place, and some of her books appear in the map key.

Map Key

 Laura and Alonzo's first home

 birthplace of Laura's sister Grace

 setting for *Little House in the Big Woods*

 setting for *Little House on the Prairie*

 setting for *The Long Winter*

 setting for *On the Banks of Plum Creek*

 Laura's house with Alonzo and daughter, Rose

1. Burr Oak is in _____.
2. The first place the Ingalls lived was in _____, _____.
3. In what town did the Ingalls live twice? _____ _____.
4. Laura wrote *Little House on the Prairie* about which city?

   _____, _____.
5. Which book was written about Walnut Grove? _____

   _____

Name_____

reading a map/area code

What's Your Area Code?

An **area code** is the three-digit code that comes before a telephone number. This code tells in which region of a state someone lives. The map below of Minnesota illustrates an area code map. Study the map and answer the questions.

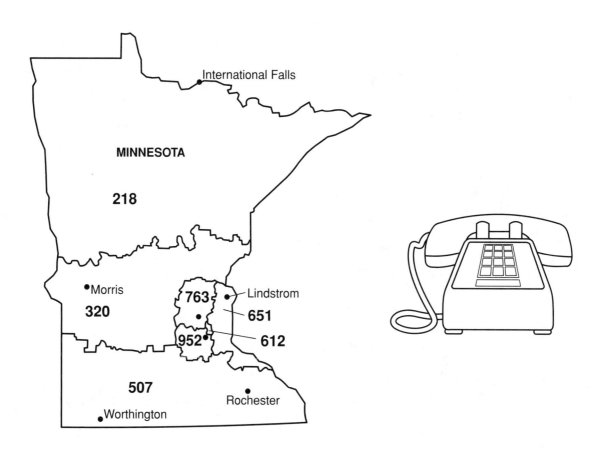

1. The area code for International Falls is ___ ___ ___.

2. Rochester and Worthington both have the ___ ___ ___ area code.

3. _____ is the only city shown on this map in the 320 area code.

4. How many area codes are given for Minnesota? _____

5. Lindstrom is in the ___ ___ ___ area code region.

© Carson-Dellosa CD-4702   Map Skills—Grade 3

Name _____

US state abbreviations

Know Your State

State abbreviations are shortened state names. On the map of the United States, study the name and shape of each state. Then, write the name of each state and its abbreviation under the correct state shape on the following pages.

Alabama	AL	Indiana	IN	Nebraska	NE	South Carolina	SC
Alaska	AK	Iowa	IA	Nevada	NV	South Dakota	SD
Arizona	AZ	Kansas	KS	New Hampshire	NH	Tennessee	TN
Arkansas	AR	Kentucky	KY	New Jersey	NJ	Texas	TX
California	CA	Louisiana	LA	New Mexico	NM	Utah	UT
Colorado	CO	Maine	ME	New York	NY	Vermont	VT
Connecticut	CT	Maryland	MD	North Carolina	NC	Virginia	VA
Delaware	DE	Massachusetts	MA	North Dakota	ND	Washington	WA
Florida	FL	Michigan	MI	Ohio	OH	West Virginia	WV
Georgia	GA	Minnesota	MN	Oklahoma	OK	Wisconsin	WI
Hawaii	HI	Mississippi	MS	Oregon	OR	Wyoming	WY
Idaho	ID	Missouri	MO	Pennsylvania	PA		

© Carson-Dellosa CD-4702   Map Skills—Grade 3

Name _____

US state abbreviations

State Abbreviations 1

1.
Name _____
Abbreviation _____

2.
Name _____
Abbreviation _____

3.
Name _____
Abbreviation _____

4.
Name _____
Abbreviation _____

5.
Name _____
Abbreviation _____

6.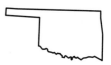
Name _____
Abbreviation _____

7.
Name _____
Abbreviation _____

8.
Name _____
Abbreviation _____

9.
Name _____
Abbreviation _____

10.
Name _____
Abbreviation _____

11.
Name _____
Abbreviation _____

12.
Name _____
Abbreviation _____

© Carson-Dellosa CD-4702   Map Skills—Grade 3

Name _____

US state abbreviations

State Abbreviations 2

13.

Name _____
Abbreviation _____

14.

Name _____
Abbreviation _____

15.

Name _____
Abbreviation _____

16.

Name _____
Abbreviation _____

17.

Name _____
Abbreviation _____

18.

Name _____
Abbreviation _____

19.

Name _____
Abbreviation _____

20.

Name _____
Abbreviation _____

21.

Name _____
Abbreviation _____

22.

Name _____
Abbreviation _____

23.

Name _____
Abbreviation _____

24.

Name _____
Abbreviation _____

© Carson-Dellosa CD-4702

Map Skills—Grade 3

Name _____

US state abbreviations

Zeke's Letters

Zeke mailed the letters below. Check his state abbreviations to see which of his letters reached the correct address. Check "Yes" if Zeke wrote the abbreviation correctly or check "no" if he wrote it incorrectly.

1. To: Aunt Polly in Arizona

   ZEKE JONES
   123 MAIN ST.
   ANYTOWN, US.

   Polly Sawyer
   411 Desert Lane
   Tucson, AO   87377

   Did Zeke's letter arrive?
   Yes   No

2. To: Anna Rose in Illinois

   ZEKE JONES
   123 MAIN ST.
   ANYTOWN, US.

   Anna Rose
   145 Bell Street
   Chicago, IL   60657

   Did Zeke's letter arrive?
   Yes   No

3. To: state representative in Texas

   ZEKE JONES
   123 MAIN ST.
   ANYTOWN, US.

   Rep. Steve Smith
   1 Capitol Drive
   Austin, TX   78767

   Did Zeke's letter arrive?

   Yes   No

4. To: Grandmother in Florida

   ZEKE JONES
   123 MAIN ST.
   ANYTOWN, US.

   Lindsay Kev
   23 Palm Tree Lane
   West Palm Beach, FA   33462

   Did Zeke's letter arrive?
   Yes   No

Name_____

US regions

Regions of the US

Sometimes maps divide countries into **regions**. Regions can be used to show climate, terrain, and many other things. The map below shows the United States divided into four major regions. Study the map and answer the questions below.

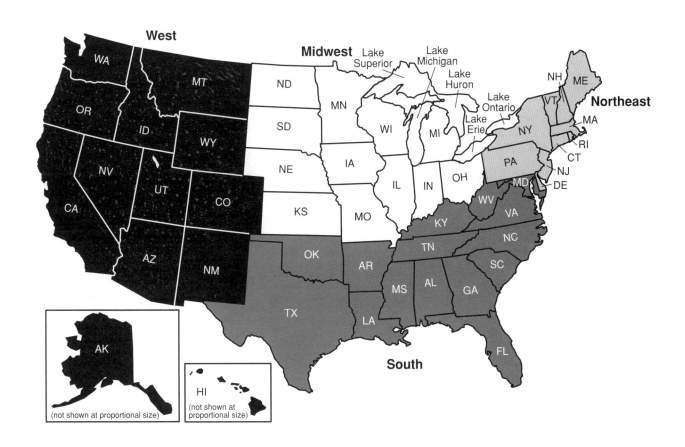

1. How many states are in the Northeast? _____
2. How many states are in the South? _____
3. Which region has the most states? _____
4. How many states are in the Midwest? _____
5. How many states are in the West? _____

© Carson-Dellosa CD-4702   Map Skills—Grade 3

Name_____

US boundaries

Boundaries within the US

Below is a map of the United States. It shows the **boundaries,** or lines, between the states. Use the map and compass rose to answer the questions below.

1. The northern boundary of Idaho (ID) and Montana (MT) is the country of _____.

2. What two states form the boundaries for South Carolina (SC)? _____ _____ and _____.

3. What state forms Colorado's (CO) western boundary? _____

4. California's (CA) northern boundary is _____.

5. Tennessee's (TN) northern boundary is _____.

© Carson-Dellosa CD-4702   22   Map Skills—Grade 3

Name_____

US cities and states

Matching Cities and States

The map below shows some large cities in the United States. Match the cities to their states by writing the correct letter from the right column in the matching blank on the left. Use an atlas if needed.

City

_____ 1. Miami
_____ 2. Denver
_____ 3. New Orleans
_____ 4. Los Angeles
_____ 5. Atlanta
_____ 6. Phoenix
_____ 7. Minneapolis
_____ 8. Seattle
_____ 9. New York

State

A. Georgia
B. Colorado
C. Minnesota
D. Louisiana
E. Washington
F. Arizona
G. California
H. Florida
I. New York

© Carson-Dellosa CD-4702   Map Skills—Grade 3

Name_____

tracing a route

Cross-Country Cycling

You are a cyclist traveling across the United States on your bicycle. Answer the questions below. Choose the shortest route between states.

What state would you travel through . . .

1. going from Ohio (OH) to Tennessee (TN)? _____
2. going from Colorado (CO) to Missouri (MO)? _____
3. going from Texas (TX) to Colorado (CO)? _____
4. going from Colorado (CO) to Montana (MT)? _____
5. going from Montana (MT) to Washington (WA)? _____
6. going from Washington (WA) to California (CA)? _____

© Carson-Dellosa CD-4702   24   Map Skills—Grade 3

Name _____

geography terms

In Terms of Geography

Below are pictures and definitions of terms used in geography. Study the pictures and read the definitions.

A **mountain** is a high, rugged landform.

A **river** is a large, natural stream of water.

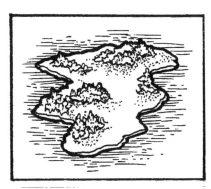

An **island** is land with water on all sides.

A **valley** is the low land between mountains.

A **plateau** is a high landform that is flat on top.

A **lake** is an inland body of water.

Oceans are the largest bodies of water on Earth.

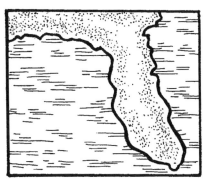

A **peninsula** is a piece of land that extends into a body of water.

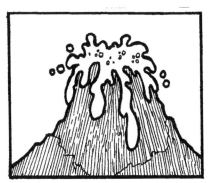

A **volcano** is land which spews forth lava from inside the earth.

© Carson-Dellosa CD-4702   25   Map Skills—Grade 3

Name_____

geography terms

Land Features

Look at the landforms in the picture. Then, draw lines to match the letter of the feature on the left to its name on the right.

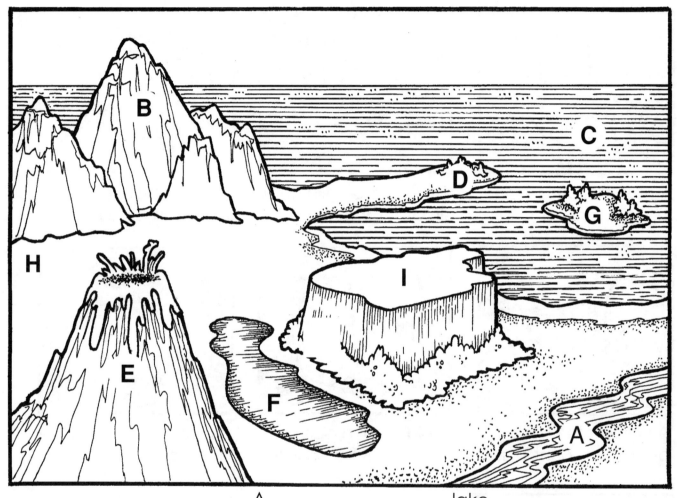

- A.   lake
- B.   river
- C.   volcano
- D.   mountain
- E.   plateau
- F.   valley
- G.   peninsula
- H.   island
- I.   ocean

Name_____

physical map

Mapping Physical Features

A **physical map** shows features such as mountains, plains, lakes, rivers, and deserts. Follow the steps below and use the map to answer the questions.

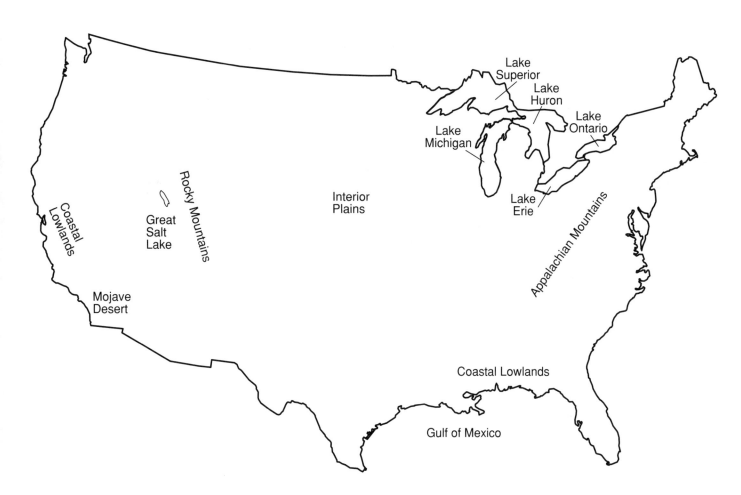

1. Underline the Appalachian Mountains and the Rocky Mountains.
2. Color the lakes blue.
3. Color the Mojave Desert brown.
4. Color the Interior Plains yellow.
5. What lake is near the Rocky Mountains?

   _____ _____ _____

6. Draw a green circle around the coastal lowlands.

Name _____

physical map

Barge and Ship Traffic

Follow the steps below to find the **routes**, or travel paths, of barges and ships in the United States.

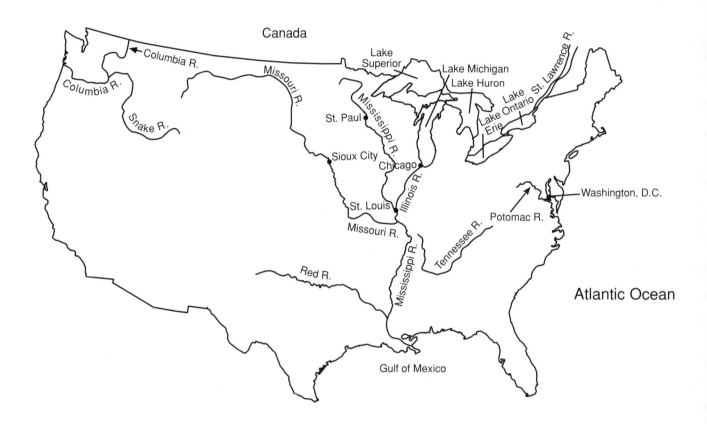

1. Color the Mississippi River route red from St. Paul to the Gulf of Mexico.
2. Color the route of a barge traveling on the Missouri River from Sioux City to the Mississippi River yellow.
3. Color the Illinois River orange from Chicago to the top of St. Louis.
4. Color the St. Lawrence River green from the Canadian border to Lake Ontario.
5. Draw a pink circle where the Potomac River meets the Atlantic Ocean.
6. Color the Snake River brown.

Name _____

product map

Precious Products

A **product map** uses symbols to show the products and resources of a region. Study the product map of Pennsylvania and answer the questions below.

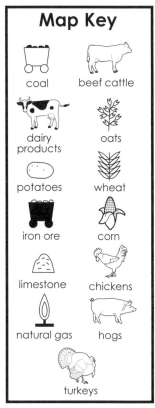
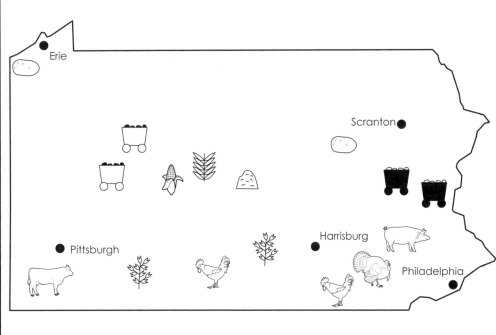

1. Which vegetable is grown near Erie? _____
2. According to the map, potatoes are grown near what cities? _____ and _____
3. Name three types of grain grown in Pennsylvania. _____, _____, and _____
4. Which two types of products are shown by cow symbols? _____ and _____ _____
5. Which three other animal products are shown on the map besides cows? _____, _____, and _____

© Carson-Dellosa CD-4702   29   Map Skills—Grade 3

Name_____

weather map

How's the Weather Up There?

Most newspapers include a **weather map** to show what the weather will be like in certain places. Weather maps can show conditions such as fog, rain, snow, and ice. Use the weather symbols on the map below to answer the questions.

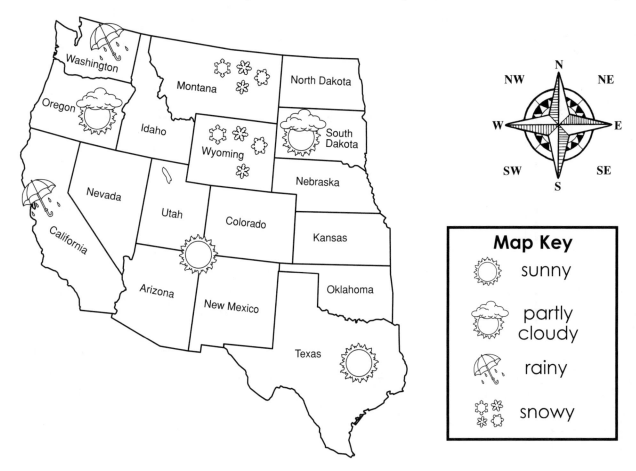

1. In which states is it rainy? _____ and _____
2. What kind of weather is Texas having? _____
3. Where could you go to find snow? _____ or _____
4. What is the weather like in South Dakota? _____ _____
5. Is it raining in Colorado? _____
6. What is the weather in Oregon? _____ _____

© Carson-Dellosa CD-4702   Map Skills—Grade 3

Name _____

US time zones

Zany Zones

The continental United States has four main **time zones**, as well as time zones for Alaska and Hawaii. Look at the time zone map below and answer the questions as if you live in New York.

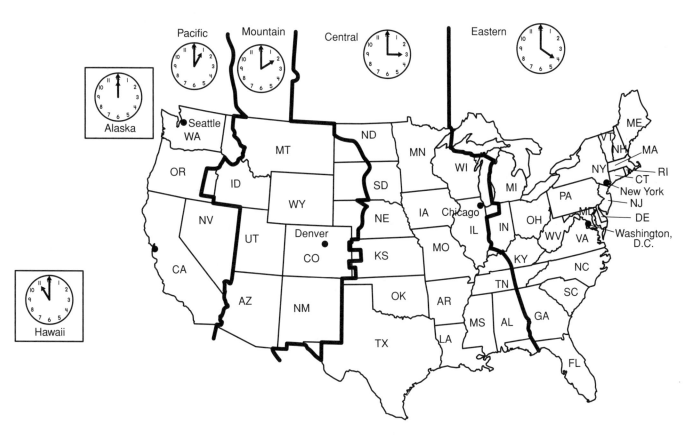

1. You live in the _____ time zone.

2. You call a friend in Denver at 8:00 A.M. eastern time. What time is it in Denver? _____

3. If your aunt in San Francisco calls at 7:00 P.M. pacific time, what time is it in New York? _____

4. A friend in Chicago needs to call your father in New York at 2:00 P.M. eastern time. What time should he call? _____

5. Your friend in Hawaii calls at 1:00 P.M. What time is it in New York? _____

Name _____

globe

Getting to Know a Globe

A **globe** is a sphere that represents Earth. The globe is divided across the middle by an imaginary line called the **equator**. The equator divides the earth into two halves, or **hemispheres**. The land and water above the equator are in the **northern hemisphere**. The land and water below the equator are in the **southern hemisphere**. The farthest point north on the globe is called the **north pole**. The point farthest south on the globe is called the **south pole**. Follow the steps below.

1. Draw a blue X on the north pole.
2. Draw a red X on the south pole.
3. The imaginary line is called the _____. Color it green.
4. Color everything in the northern hemisphere yellow.
5. Color everything in the southern hemisphere orange.

© Carson-Dellosa CD-4702

Name_____

hemispheres

East and West

Study the map to the right. Write the name of each continent beside its letter below. You may use an atlas.

A. _ _ _ _ _   _ _ _ _ _ _ _
   1 2   3   4

B. _ _ _ _ _   _ _ _ _ _ _ _
   5   6   7

C. _ _ _ _ _ _ _ _ _ _
       8

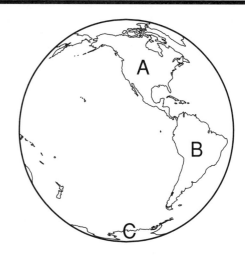

Use the letter code above to solve the puzzle below. The continents above (or parts of them) are found in the:

W _ _ _ _ _ _   _ _ _ _ _   P _ _ _ _
   7 5 8 7 2 1   6 7 3 4 5   6 7 2 7

Study the map to the right. Write the name of each continent beside its letter below. You may use an atlas.

A. _ _ _ _ _ _
   1   2

B. _ _ _ _
    3

C. _ _ _ _ _ _
   4 5

D. _ _ _ _ _ _ _ _ _
      6

E. _ _ _ _ _ _ _ _ _
       7

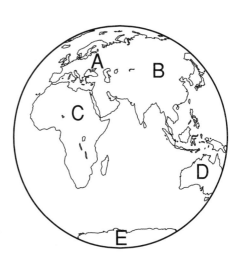

Use the letter code above to solve the puzzle below. The continents above (or parts of them) are found in the:

_ _ _ _ _ _ N   H _ M _ _ _ H _ _ _
1 4 3 6 1 5   1   7 3 2 1 5 1

© Carson-Dellosa CD-4702   33   Map Skills—Grade 3

Name_____

introducing latitude

Round and Round

Lines of latitude are imaginary lines that run east to west on a map. They are marked in **degrees**. The **equator** is 0° latitude. The lines of latitude on the globe below are measured in 15° segments from the equator. Places north of the equator have the letter "N" after their degrees. Places south of the equator have the letter "S" after their degrees. Look at the map and answer the questions.

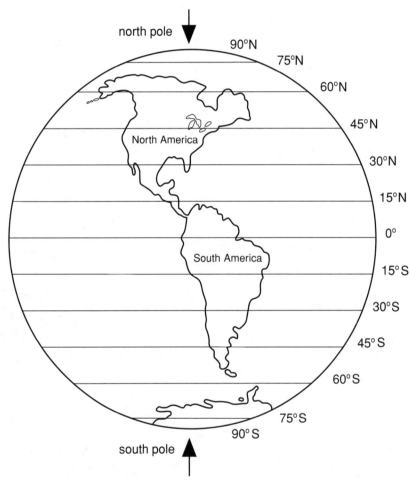

1. The equator is _____° latitude.
2. For locations in North America, the latitude should be followed by the letter _____.
3. The latitude for the southern tip of South America would be followed by the letter _____.
4. Use a red crayon to trace the equator.

© Carson-Dellosa CD-4702

Map Skills—Grade 3

Name_____

introducing longitude

Up and Down

Lines of longitude are imaginary lines that run north to south on a map. They are marked in **degrees**. The prime meridian is 0° longitude. The lines of longitude on the globe below are measured in 15° segments from the prime meridian. Places east of the prime meridian have the letter "E" after their degrees. Places west of the prime meridian have the letter "W" after their degrees.

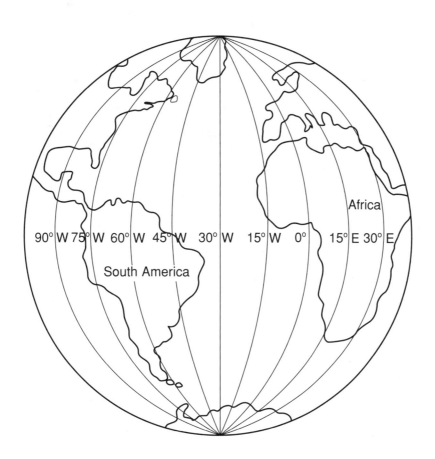

1. The prime meridian is _____° longitude.
2. For locations in South America, the longitude should be followed by the letter _____.
3. For locations in most of Africa, the longitude should be followed by the letter _____.
4. Use an orange crayon to trace the prime meridian.

© Carson-Dellosa CD-4702   Map Skills—Grade 3

Name_____

latitude/longitude

Hailey's Report

Hailey wants to find out the latitude and longitude for several large cities. Use the map below to find out which cities she researched. Write the names of the cities in the blanks below.

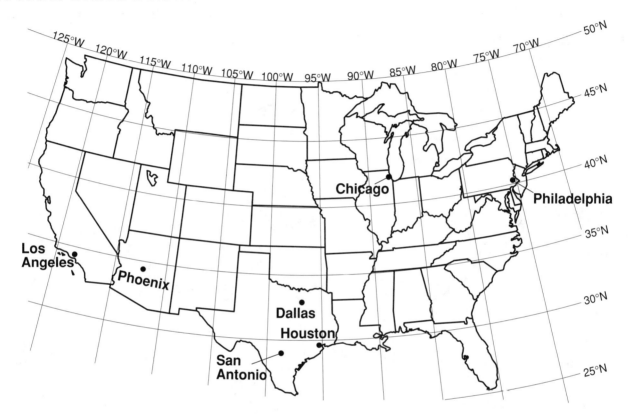

Latitude	Longitude	City
1. 34°N	118°W	_____
2. 42°N	87°W	_____
3. 29°N	95°W	_____
4. 41°N	75°W	_____
5. 34°N	112°W	_____
6. 33°N	96°W	_____
7. 29°N	98°W	_____

© Carson-Dellosa CD-4702 36 Map Skills—Grade 3

Name _____

locating countries

Jeffrey's Stamp Collection

Jeffrey collects stamps. He has stamps from six different countries. Find and color each country from which Jeffrey has a stamp. Color each stamp and its matching country the same color.

© Carson-Dellosa CD-4702   37   Map Skills—Grade 3

Name_____

continents

Mixed-Up Continents

There are seven **continents**, or large land masses, on Earth. The graph below compares the amount of land area of each continent. Use the graph to answer the questions.

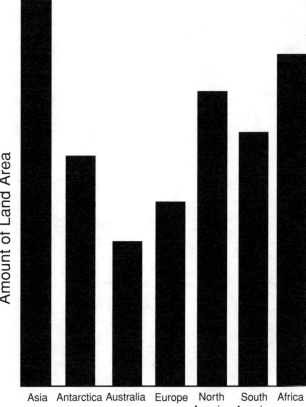

Write the continents in order by size, from smallest to largest.

1. _____
2. _____
3. _____
4. _____
5. _____
6. _____
7. _____

Write the continents in alphabetical order.

1. _____
2. _____
3. _____
4. _____
5. _____
6. _____
7. _____

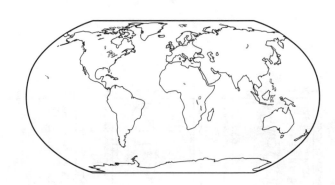

© Carson-Dellosa CD-4702   38   Map Skills—Grade 3

Name_____

cities/countries/continents

Cities, Countries, Continents

Political maps show land masses divided into regions such as **continents**, **countries**, and **cities**. Study a world map in an atlas. Look at the list of regions below. Match the regions below by drawing lines to connect the cities to their countries, and the countries to their continents.

City	**Country**	**Continent**
Cairo	Australia	South America
Lima	Canada	Europe
Beijing	Egypt	Asia
Paris	China	Australia
Montreal	Peru	North America
Sydney	France	Africa

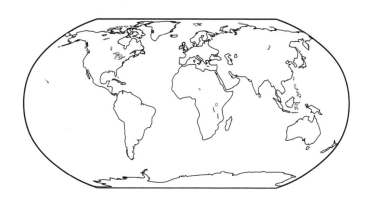

© Carson-Dellosa CD-4702   Map Skills—Grade 3

Name_____

political map

Cities and Countries

Below is a political map of the continent of South America. The map shows the countries of South America and some of the cities in each country. Color each of the countries on the map a different color. Then, circle the city names.

© Carson-Dellosa CD-4702

Map Skills—Grade 3

Name_____

oceans

Earth's Oceans

Oceans are bodies of water that cover large areas of Earth. There are four oceans. The bar graph below shows their sizes. Color the oceans blue on the world map. Then, list the four oceans from largest to smallest in the blanks below.

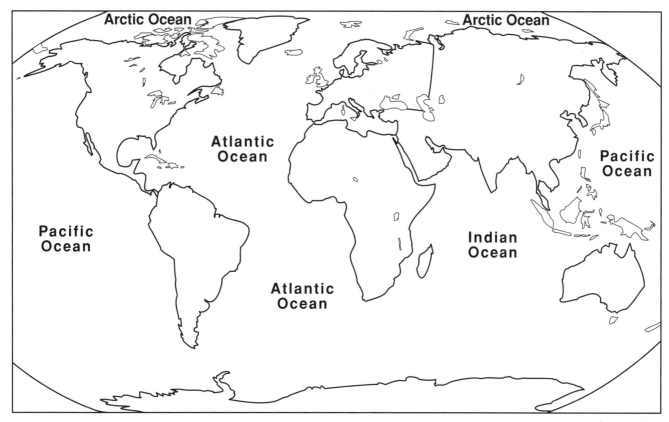

1. _____

2. _____

3. _____

4. _____

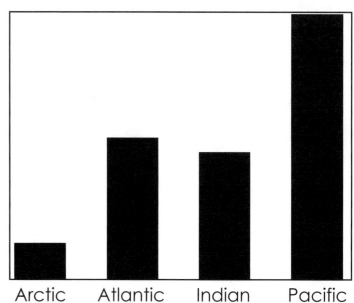

Name_____

review

Matching Maps

You have learned about political maps, physical maps, weather maps, globes, the compass rose, and floor plans. Match each picture below with its name by writing the correct letter from the list in the blank beside the picture.

_____ 1.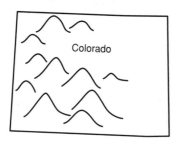

_____ 2.

_____ 3.

_____ 4.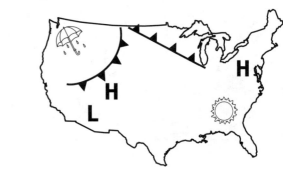

_____ 5.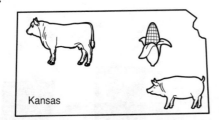

_____ 6.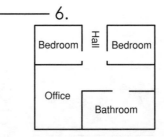

A. product map
B. globe
C. political map

D. weather map
E. physical map
F. floor plan

© Carson-Dellosa CD-4702   42   Map Skills—Grade 3

Name _____

review

Map Skills Review

The questions below review the map skills you have learned. Read each question and fill in the blank with a word from the word bank below.

1. This tool is used to show direction on a map. _____

2. This shows the unit used to measure distance on a map. _____

3. These are letters and numbers used with a grid to show where a location is on a map. _____

4. Its location on the globe is 0° latitude. _____

5. Its location on the globe is 0° longitude. _____ _____

6. Half of the globe is called a _____.

7. This is a political division of a continent. The United States is one. _____

8. Numbers for a specific region used in front of a phone number. _____ _____

9. The lines that run east to west on a map: lines of _____

10. The lines that run north to south on a map: lines of _____

11. There are four of these large bodies of water on Earth. _____

12. This kind of map shows land and water features of a region. _____ _____

13. There are seven of these land masses on Earth. _____

Word Bank

longitude	hemisphere	prime meridian
latitude	oceans	equator
country	compass rose	scale
coordinates	area code	continents
	physical map	

Name_____

review

Word Search

Find the words listed in the word bank on page 43 in the puzzle. Words can appear horizontally, vertically, diagonally, or backwards.

```
C B W T X R O E S S M D O E C V W Z R L
O O L O C T R S V X O O M J K C B A K N
N S M T A R M N L A Z P E D O C A E R A
T A R P O S T A L C O D E E D D C W P I
I B R I A S R T N E F U Q Z G J A S T D
N M O N S S C A L E E L U M P C I Y S I
E L A R R B S C O V R E A W A B A S T R
N T R E N K R R L L E I T V M W V O U E
T A A S N A E C O C C P O V L O M S T M
S C E N P M S E R S T T R U A V V Z Y E
Y O V J K T E A N S E E D E C S S M O M
R J C D W V Y Y S S E D I S I R R S T I
T T O N K J L E E F U R N I S S U W Q R
E Q A U E K L D C C O Y E W Y Z A O U P
D A R J K E U S S M R Z O H H C A S P O
U R S S S T D A Z T L L K R P N N I J P
T W B V I Q A E N S N T E L X S N O S N
I S S G B L E U I J M A N T A R I S S E
T O N O A C O V X O O S B E R N T M A A
A O E G I C O O R D I N A T E S L P E O
L L A S R E V P R E E N T S S B B E D H
```

Map of the United States

Answer Key

Jacob's Neighborhood (pg. 5)
1. north
2. west
3. east
4. northeast
5. northwest

Following Directions (pg. 6)
Check to make sure that students have marked the map according to the directions. The finishing point is the bottom right corner.

The Old West (pg. 7)
1. $
2. hotel
3. bank
4. blacksmith
5. horse stables

Craft Fair (pg. 8)

Lacey's Laundry (pg. 9)

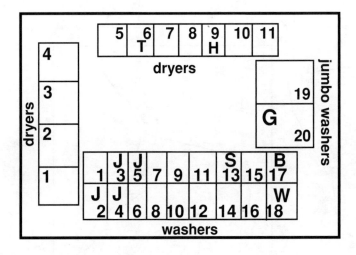

My Map (pg. 10)
Maps will vary. Check to make sure that students have labeled the compass rose.

Stargazer (pg. 11)

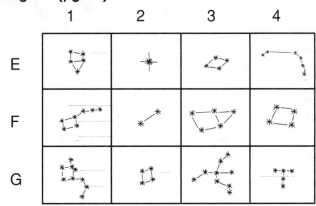

Wonder Cave (pg. 12)
1. A-2
2. C-2
3. D-3
4. C-3
5. B-2
6. B-3
7. B-4

African Safari (pg. 13)
1. 55
2. 25
3. 80
4. 50

How Far? (pg. 14)
1. no
2. St. Louis Arch
3. Space Needle
4. 1,200 miles

Places Laura Lived (pg. 15)
1. Iowa
2. Pepin, Wisconsin
3. Walnut Grove
4. Independence, Kansas
5. *On the Banks of Plum Creek*

What's Your Area Code? (pg. 16)
1. 218
2. 507
3. Morris
4. 7
5. 651

Know Your State (pg. 17)
Check to make sure that students have labeled the map correctly.

© Carson-Dellosa CD-4702 — Map Skills—Grade 3

Answer Key

State Abbreviations 1 & 2 (pgs. 18-19)
1. Washington, WA
2. Georgia, GA
3. Wisconsin, WI
4. New York, NY
5. Alabama, AL
6. Oklahoma, OK
7. Michigan, MI
8. Maine, ME
9. Maryland, MD
10. West Virginia, WV
11. Florida, FL
12. Montana, MT
13. Arizona, AZ
14. Delaware, DE
15. Nebraska, NE
16. Alaska, AK
17. Oregon, OR
18. Massachusetts, MA
19. Minnesota, MN
20. Kentucky, KY
21. New Mexico, NM
22. Mississippi, MS
23. South Carolina, SC
24. Missouri, MO

Zeke's Letters (pg. 20)
The following boxes should be checked:
1. no
2. yes
3. yes
4. no

Regions of the US (pg. 21)
1. 10
2. 15
3. South
4. 12
5. 13

Boundaries within the US (pg. 22)
1. Canada
2. North Carolina, Georgia
3. Utah
4. Oregon
5. Kentucky

Matching Cities and States (pg. 23)
1. H
2. B
3. D
4. G
5. A
6. F
7. C
8. E
9. I

Cross-Country Cycling (pg. 24)
1. Kentucky
2. Kansas
3. Oklahoma
4. Wyoming
5. Idaho
6. Oregon

Land Features (pg. 26)
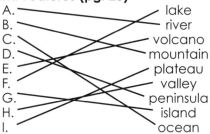

Mapping Physical Features (pg. 27)
Check to make sure that students have marked the map according to the directions.
5. Great Salt Lake

Barge and Ship Traffic (pg. 28)
Check to make sure all paths are colored correctly and a pink circle is drawn where the Potomac River meets the Atlantic Ocean.

Precious Products (pg. 29)
1. potatoes
2. Erie, Scranton
3. oats, wheat, corn
4. beef cattle, dairy products
5. chickens, hogs, turkeys

How's the Weather Up There? (pg. 30)
1. California, Washington
2. sunny
3. Wyoming, Montana
4. partly cloudy
5. no
6. partly cloudy

Zany Zones (pg. 31)
1. eastern
2. 6:00 A.M.
3. 10:00 P.M.
4. 1:00 P.M.
5. 6:00 P.M.

Getting to Know a Globe (pg. 32)
3. equator

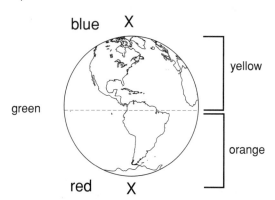

East and West (pg. 33)
A. North America
B. South America
C. Antarctica
western hemisphere

A. Europe
B. Asia
C. Africa
D. Australia
E. Antarctica
eastern hemisphere

Answer Key

Round and Round (pg. 34)
1. 0
2. N
3. S
4. Check to make sure that students have traced the equator with red.

Up and Down (pg. 35)
1. 0
2. W
3. E
4. Check to make sure that students have traced the prime meridian with orange.

Hailey's Report (pg. 36)
1. Los Angeles
2. Chicago
3. Houston
4. Philadelphia
5. Phoenix
6. Dallas
7. San Antonio

Jeffrey's Stamp Collection (pg. 37)
Check to make sure that the stamps have been colored the same as their corresponding countries.

Mixed-Up Continents (pg. 38)
Continents by size:
1. Australia
2. Europe
3. Antarctica
4. South America
5. North America
6. Africa
7. Asia

Continents in alphabetical order:
1. Africa
2. Antarctica
3. Asia
4. Australia
5. Europe
6. North America
7. South America

Cities, Countries, Continents (pg. 39)

City	Country	Continent
Cairo	Australia	South America
Lima	Canada	Europe
Beijing	Egypt	Asia
Paris	China	Australia
Montreal	Peru	North America
Sydney	France	Africa

(lines matching each city to its country and continent)

Cities and Countries (pg. 40)
Check to make sure that students have colored each country a different color and circled city names.

Earth's Oceans (pg. 41)
1. Pacific
2. Atlantic
3. Indian
4. Arctic

Check to make sure that students have colored the oceans blue.

Matching Maps (pg. 42)
1. E
2. C
3. B
4. D
5. A
6. F

Map Skills Review (pg. 43)
1. compass rose
2. scale
3. coordinates
4. equator
5. prime meridian
6. hemisphere
7. country
8. area code
9. latitude
10. longitude
11. oceans
12. physical map
13. continents

Word Search (pg. 44)

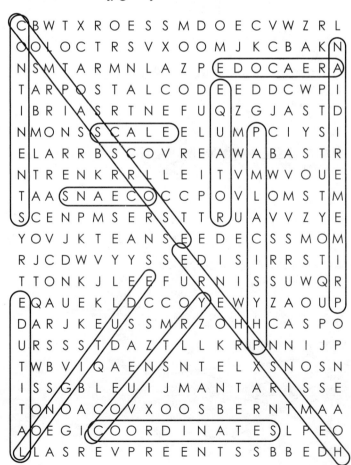

© Carson-Dellosa CD-4702   48   Map Skills—Grade 3